AFRICAN AMERICAN LEADERS FIGHT FOR FREEDOM

Frederick Douglass and Sojourner Truth

Black Biographies Grade 5 | Children's Biographies

DISSECTED LIVES
auto biographies

First Edition, 2021

Published in the United States by Speedy Publishing LLC, 40 E Main Street, Newark, Delaware 19711 USA.

10 9 8 7 6 * 5 4 3 2 1

Print Edition: 9781541960527
Digital Edition: 9781541963528
Hardcover Edition: 9781541986435

TABLE OF CONTENTS

The institution of slavery was so horrific that throughout the 1800s, many people spoke out against it. Hearing passionate speeches by white Americans could stir audiences to support the cause. However, hearing the powerful messages of former slaves speaking about their actual experiences could shine a spotlight on the evils of enslavement. Two former slaves, Frederick Douglass and Sojourner Truth, gained their freedom and used their experience to help the abolitionist movement. Let's learn about the extraordinary lives of Frederick Douglass and Sojourner Truth and how they devoted their lives to push the abolitionist cause.

Frederick Douglass and Sojourner Truth

THE ABOLITIONIST MOVEMENT

William Lloyd Garrison

Although the ethics of slavery have been debated for much longer, the movement to abolish slavery in the United States really gained momentum in 1831. On January 1 of that year, William Lloyd Garrison printed the first edition of his new periodical. It was a weekly newsletter called *The Liberator*.

The Liberator was published weekly until 1865, after the Civil War was over. The publication of this newsletter kickstarted the abolitionist movement. At this time, there was a shift in the collective thought of the American public. People became more aware of the disparities between themselves and other groups, like African American slaves. The general attitude was that tremendous social reforms were needed in the country.

The front page of "The Liberator" from April 11, 1845.

THE LIBERATOR

OUR COUNTRY IS THE WORLD--OUR COUNTRYMEN ARE ALL MANKIND.

BOSTON, FRIDAY, APRIL 11, 1845.

BERATOR.

M HENRY C. WRIGHT.

July 12, 1845. 9 o'clock, A. M.

Market.

nota. The market full of the ne country round, with a great ild and domestic animals, and of all kinds. The most abundant *nectarine*; and cheap, three and cent, in value. Every thing is any one going hungry or cold market-house—the buying and e open air, on benches and ta- ide-walks, and around and in a appearance of the people im- ably, as to their social and do- le who appear so neat and tidy ially the *sellers*, must have com- homes. Their dress, especially , is most singular. Instead of tastically about their heads, in omen of Salzburgh and Linz, or on of Scotland and Ireland, the nly wear *hats*, like the men, or r cotton, dyed blue, and running people from the country, with are mostly women, and many two young children as helpers. stians, with their wares, and sev- ls, where they are busy, display- udging from their appearance in l think the Tyrolese a much more ng people, than those of Austria —more sprightly and active in d habits—more shrewd. This is ich an unusual gathering is seen main-street is filled with men, wo- ll seeming eager to sell or to buy. disposition, evidently, to make uy cheap and sell dear—the busi- whole world. I have just pur- tarines, and had a very pleasant . There is no place like a mar- acter of a people. I have now ooking at every thing and every busy scene with regret.

12 *o'clock, noon.*

16th, 17th and 18th centuries in this church, so far as men and things are concerned; for it seems to be the great object of the church to throw around those men and deeds of violence and blood, the sanctions of Christianity. It is most melancholy to stand amid this church, and see the characters of those who have contested the destinies of Europe for the last 400 years. They have been distinguished only for their vices and villany. These national, public adulterers, robbers and murderers, must ere long be brought to the same test to which the private individual is brought. My regard for what are called holy times, places and callings, is all gone. This gloomy old building really seems to me, with all its decorations of pulpits, altars, organs and pictures, like a den of thieves and robbers. I know holy men and women, but I know no holy days, pulpits, or houses. All days are the Lord's days—all places, the Lord's places. In this church, Christiana, Queen of Sweden, was received into the Catholic church in 1655—on which occasion there was a great gathering of priests and people, and great shoutings and rejoicings.

Now in the Museum.

In one division is the Picture Gallery—the pictures principally the work of Tyrolese artists. In another room is a large collection of the natural productions of Tyrol—minerals and fossils—some fine specimens of gold. A fine Herbarium, devoted to the various and beautiful flowers of the Tyrol. Here I see collected specimens of all the mineral and vegetable productions of this interesting country. Another room is devoted to the works of art. The carved *wood-work* is most interesting. Here are most beautiful specimens of iron and steel ware, cutlery, tools and implements of all kinds. The Tyrolese are a most ingenious people; and if their country could, by means of railroads or canals, be connected with other countries with which they could carry on commerce, they might soon come to compete with any other nation in all kinds of manufactures. Nothing can exceed the beauty of the specimens of silk, wood and iron work in this room. In the room in which I now am is the *Library*. Not many books of value, but several manuscripts of interest. Have just read the original letter of Lord Bathurst, the British Foreign Secretary in 1810, to Hofer and the Tyrolese, accompanied by a draft of $150,000, (£30,000) from the English Government, to aid them in carrying on the war against Napoleon—and ...

For the Rochester Advertiser.

THE AMERICAN UNION.

FRIEND HUMPHREY:

Having noticed in the Advertiser of Saturday morning, an article on 'the slave question,' I venture to offer a few remarks on the same subject, supposing your paper is free enough to allow a short comment on one of its editorials. In doing so, I shall not, to any great extent, comment directly upon your article, for the most of it is so plain as to 'speak for itself.' It is not to be wondered at that editors of party papers should make some singular mistakes when they speak of this subject.

First, then, I will give a brief answer to your question, 'What would the severance of the Union do?' by giving you the opinion of some of our Southern brethren themselves; and all will probably allow that they know *as well*, at least, as those who do not own human beings. The editor of the Maysville (Tenn.) Intelligencer, speaking of the condition and character of the slave population, says: 'But the consciousness, with all their stupidity, that a ten-fold force, superior in discipline, if not in barbarity, would gather from the four corners of the United States, and slaughter them, keeps them in subjection.—☞ *But to the non-slaveholding States, particularly, we are indebted for a permanent safeguard against insurrection.* ☜ Without their assistance, the white population of the South would be *too weak* to quiet that innate desire for liberty which is ever ready to act itself out with every rational creature.' Underwood of Kentucky said, when speaking, in his place in Congress, on the famous Haverhill dissolution petition, '*The dissolution of the Union is the destruction of slavery.* * * * If the Union were divided into two parts, the slave would cross the line, and then turn round and curse his master from the other shore. Arnold of Tennessee, on the same subject, said—'Suppose the dissolution could be peaceably effected, (if that did not involve a contradiction in terms,) what had the South to depend upon? *All the crowned heads were against her. A million of slaves were ready to rise, and strike at the first tap of the drum.* They were cut loose from their friends at the North, (friends that ought to be, and without them the South had [illegible] * Whither were they to look for protect[illegible] were they to sustain an assault from Eng[illegible]ance, with that cancer in their vitals? The [illegible] South reflected, the more clearly she [illegible] she had a deep and vital interest in

From the Herald of Freedom.

NEW-HAMPSHIRE ANTI-SLAVERY.

THE PAST AND PRESENT.

It is well at times to take a view of the past. No revolution in the whole progress of man, will afford more ample, or more important material for the pen of the historian, than that now waging in this country between the friends and foes of genuine Liberty. Unlike the revolutions of past ages, its course is not marked with carnage and blood. Let this land congratulate itself that the principle actors in the great moral drama, that gives character and glory to the age, are not, like the teachers and supporters of the national religion, the worshippers of a God of battles, but of a Prince of peace. No 'confused noise of battle and' garments rolled in blood,' mark their course. No Bunker Hill strewed with corpses of the slain—no plains of Belgium steeped in the blood of tens of thousands—no shrieks of dying hosts,—no wail of widows nor woe of orphans attend their goings, and clothe all nature and humanity in sackcloth. They come as the angels to the shepherds on Judea's plains, proclaiming peace on earth, good will to men. Long ages of fearful night has fell Oppression swayed his iron septre, and kept horrid festival on the blood and tears of untold generations. On that dread night they break, peaceful and serene, as dawn of morning. 'Theirs is the sword of the spirit, the word of truth. They break not the arm, but melt the heart of the oppressor. They shed not his blood, but would soften his spirit. They point him to his victim, bruised and wounded at his feet, and say, 'Behold thy brother.' They come not to destroy men's lives, but to save them. Their mission is, to seek and save that which was lost.

But it was of the progress the cause of Freedom is making among the fastnesses of the Granite State that I was to speak. It may be my vision is perverted; but a glance at things as they appear, has filled me with sadness for the condition of our enterprise. Five years ago, and we were mighty in numerical strength. But the cholera of New Organization made fearful havoc among our hosts.

A remnant, however, was saved. With that remnant, we again fearlessly entered the lists. The year 1841 was one continued series of victorious conquests. At the annual meeting in 1840, the enemy, headed by the clergy, made their final onset: But it was to them a fatal hour. From that period, we date our attack on the 'bulwarks of slavery,' and it has since been, on our part, a war not of defence, but of aggression. While the then Editor of the Herald of Freedom was in Great Britain, the paper assumed the ground, that our churches were no longer worthy of support. It declared the time had come '*to cease calling gangs of man-stealers, Christian churches.*' It asserted that 'the name no more

THE SLAVERY OF FREDERICK DOUGLASS

Born into slavery, Frederick Douglass was born sometime in February of 1818, but the exact date of his birth was not recorded.

Frederick Douglass

Historians believe he was born in his grandmother's on a plantation on the shores of the Chesapeake Bay in Maryland. It is most likely that Douglass's father was a white man, perhaps the master of the plantation. Douglass and his mother were kept apart. He was raised by his grandmother, Betsy Bailey. She was also a slave.

Frederick Douglass was believed to be born on a plantation in Wye house in Easton, Maryland.

FREEMEN VERSUS SLAVES

Thomas Auld

Frederick Douglass was taken from his grandmother when he was six years old. He went first to the Wye House Plantation and then to Thomas and Lucretia Auld of Baltimore.

In the city, the young Frederick Douglass first encountered free blacks and began to understand his servitude. He compared the lives of the freemen in the city with the lives of the slaves on the plantations. It was then that he vowed to become a free man himself.

Wye House, American plantation.

AN EARLY EDUCATION

Mrs. Auld teaching young Frederick how to read.

Sophia Auld, the sister-in-law of his master, taught Frederick Douglass how to read and write beginning when he was about 12 years old. She took an interest in the young slave boy. For example, she made sure Douglass was properly fed. She made sure he had a good bed to sleep in and nice clothes to wear.

Later, as an adult, Douglass would explain that Sophia Auld showed him how one human being was supposed to treat another. Her husband, however, disapproved of the lessons she gave the boy. He told his wife that educating black people would only result in them wanting their freedom.

Thomas Auld did not approve of his wife educating Frederick.

Holy Bible

Sophia Auld stopped tutoring Douglass, but he never stopped learning. Armed with a basic knowledge of reading and writing, Douglass taught himself by reading everything he could get his hands on.

Douglass never stopped learning.

THE SLAVERY OF SOJOURNER TRUTH

Isabella Baumfree

Sojourner Truth changed her name when she became free. She was born Isabella Baumfree in 1797, one of a dozen children of James and Elizabeth Baumfree.

When she was young, the slave owner kept her entire family together, but when he died, the children were auctioned off at a slave auction. Nine-year-old Sojourner Truth was sold to John Neely, a cruel and abusive slave owner. She was sold to yet another abusive owner. The owner's wife also made Truth's life miserable.

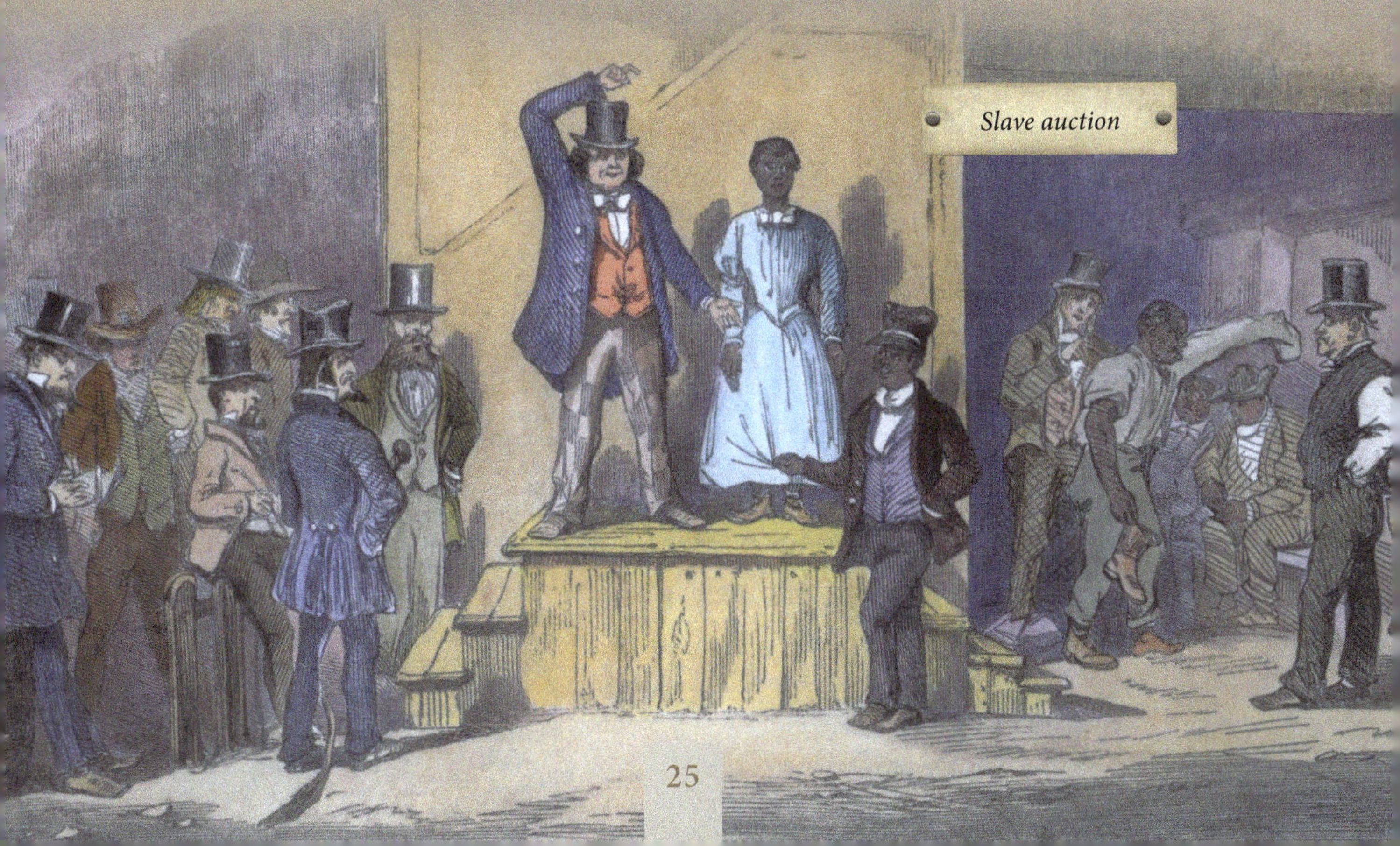

Slave auction

SOJOURNER
TRUTH IN LOVE

In 1815, when she was around 18 years old, Sojourner Truth began a romantic relationship with a slave from a neighboring farm. His name was Robert. Robert's owner, however, did not want the couple together. If they had children together, Robert's owner would not own the children. They would be the property of Sojourner's owner.

Young Isabella

Robert was caught sneaking and was nearly beaten to death.

One time, Robert's owner caught him sneaking over to see Sojourner. Robert was mercilessly beaten and nearly died from his injuries. The broken-hearted Sojourner never saw him again. She was deeply impacted by the incident. Later, Sojourner married a slave from her own farm named Thomas and had five children.

FREDERICK DOUGLASS'S PATH TO FREEDOM

Frederick Douglass met Anna Murray, a free black woman, in 1837. The two fell in love and wanted to marry, however that was impossible because Douglass was a slave. The only way for the couple to be together was for Douglass to escape slavery.

He hopped on a train heading north on September 3, 1838. The train took him to Philadelphia. Anna Murray had given him travel money. She also provided him with a sailor uniform and identification papers stating that he was a free black sailor.

Douglass escaped slavery.

NEW ENGLAND

From Philadelphia, he continued on to New York City to a safe house. He sent a letter to Anna Murray to let her know he had arrived in New York City. She soon joined him. They were married on September 15, 1838, less than two weeks after Douglass escaped slavery.

Douglass and Murray were married on September 15, 1838.

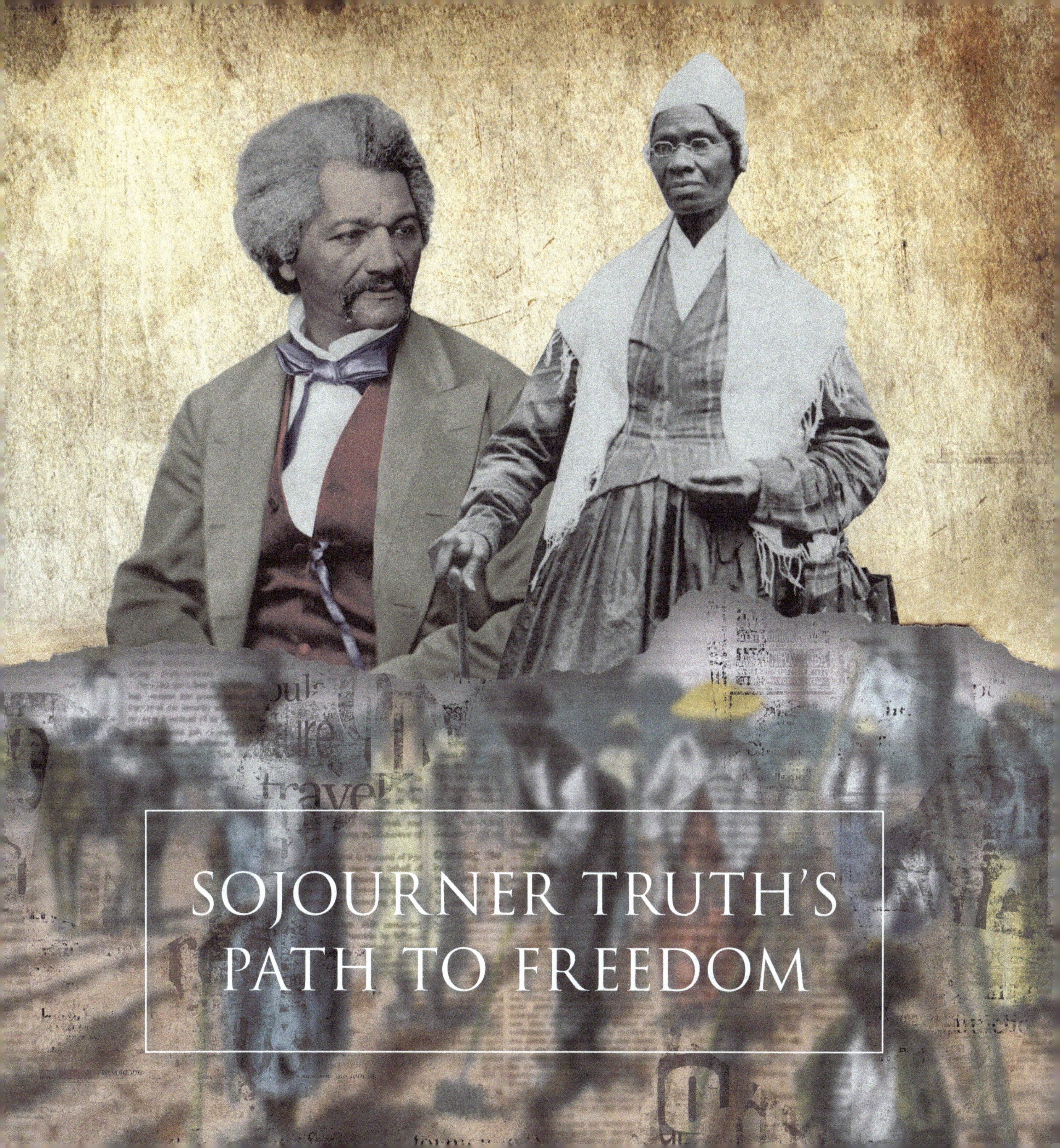

SOJOURNER TRUTH'S PATH TO FREEDOM

Sojourner Truth was a slave in New York State. On July 4, 1827, the state planned to free all the slaves living there and abolish slavery. About six months prior to this, Sojourner Truth took her youngest child who was just an infant and simply walked away from her owner's farm. She could not take her other children with her because they could not be freed, under the upcoming state emancipation law. They would have to wait until they reached adulthood.

Sojourner Truth took her infant and walked away from her owner.

Sojourner Truth and her baby were taken in by Isaac and Maria Van Wagenen who allowed her to stay with them until the state emancipation took place and Truth was free.

Isaac and Maria Van Wagenen

FREEING HER SON

While living with the Van Wagenen's, Sojourner Truth heard that her five-year-old son, Peter, had been illegally sold to a Southern plantation owner and sent to Alabama. Isaac Van Wagenen encouraged Truth to file legal action against her former owner to get her son back.

Sojourner filed legal action to get her son back.

The court case took several months to settle, but Truth won her case and got her son back. This was one of the first times that an African American woman won a legal case against a white man.

Sojourner Truth won the case and got her son back.

FREDERICK DOUGLASS AND THE ABOLITIONIST MOVEMENT

Frederick Douglass and his wife moved to New Bedford, Massachusetts. This area was popular among former slaves and had become a center for the abolitionist movement. The couple joined a church and Douglass served as a preacher. An educated former slave was a bit of a novelty in those days.

Home of Frederick Douglass and his wife in New Bedford, Massachusetts.

Douglass honed his speaking skills and continued to read as much as he could. His favorite newspaper was The Liberator. Douglass was asked to deliver a speech at the annual meeting of the Massachusetts Anti-Slavery Society. He spoke emotionally about his life in slavery. The success of that speech led to more invitations to speak on behalf of the abolitionist movement. He embarked on a six-month speaking tour in 1843. He joined several other notable speakers and gave speeches across the northern part of the United States.

Frederick Douglass speaking in England on his experiences as a slave.

SOJOURNER TRUTH AND THE ABOLITIONIST MOVEMENT

Sojourner Truth had a religious experience. Afterwards, she felt called to help others. She traveled to New Bedford, Massachusetts. There, she attracted large crowds of followers with her fiery speeches, passionate preaching, and even her singing.

Sojourner Truth, African-American abolitionist and women's rights activist.

She joined an organization, called the Northampton Association of Education and Industry in 1844. This was a group founded by abolitionists to promote the rights of former slaves and women. While working with this group, Sojourner Truth met other abolitionists, including Frederick Douglass.

Headquarters of the Northampton Association of Education and Industry (NAEI) in Massachusetts

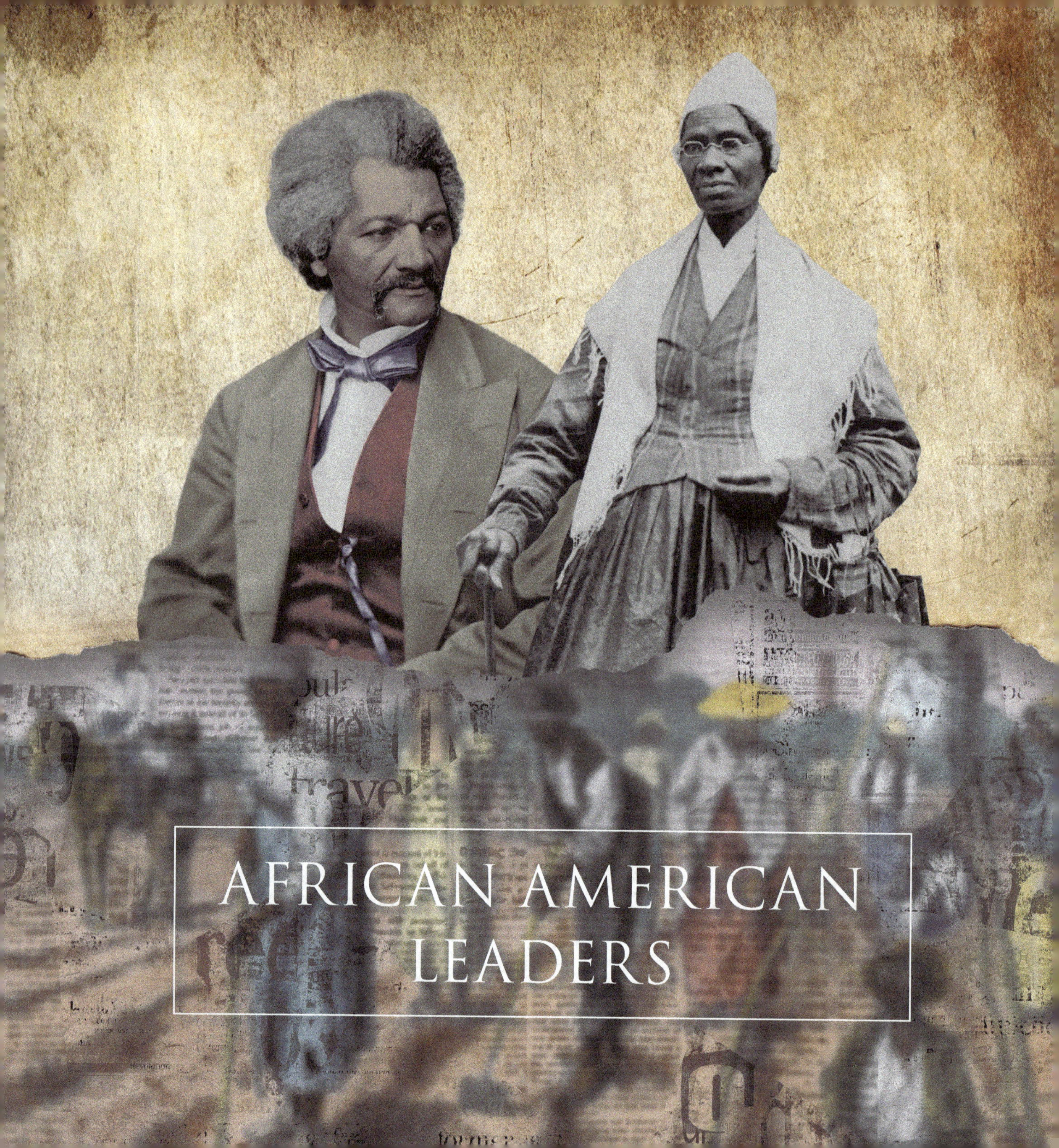

AFRICAN AMERICAN LEADERS

Frederick Douglass and Sojourner Truth

Frederick Douglass was one of several people who encouraged Sojourner Truth to give speeches to support the abolitionist cause. While Douglass admired Truth's rousing style of speaking, he looked down on her for her lack of education. Truth never learned to read or write.

Douglass believed that the key to empowering the African American people was through education. Still, both Douglass and Truth were powerful African American leaders. Truth worked on behalf of all underprivileged people, especially blacks and women.

Douglass believed that education is the key to freedom.

LASTING LITERATURE

One of Sojourner Truth's most memorable speeches was titled, "Ain't I a Woman." She gave this speech at a women's convention in Ohio. In her speech, Truth demanded equal rights for all women, black and white. She used her platform as a former slave to reinforce her views.

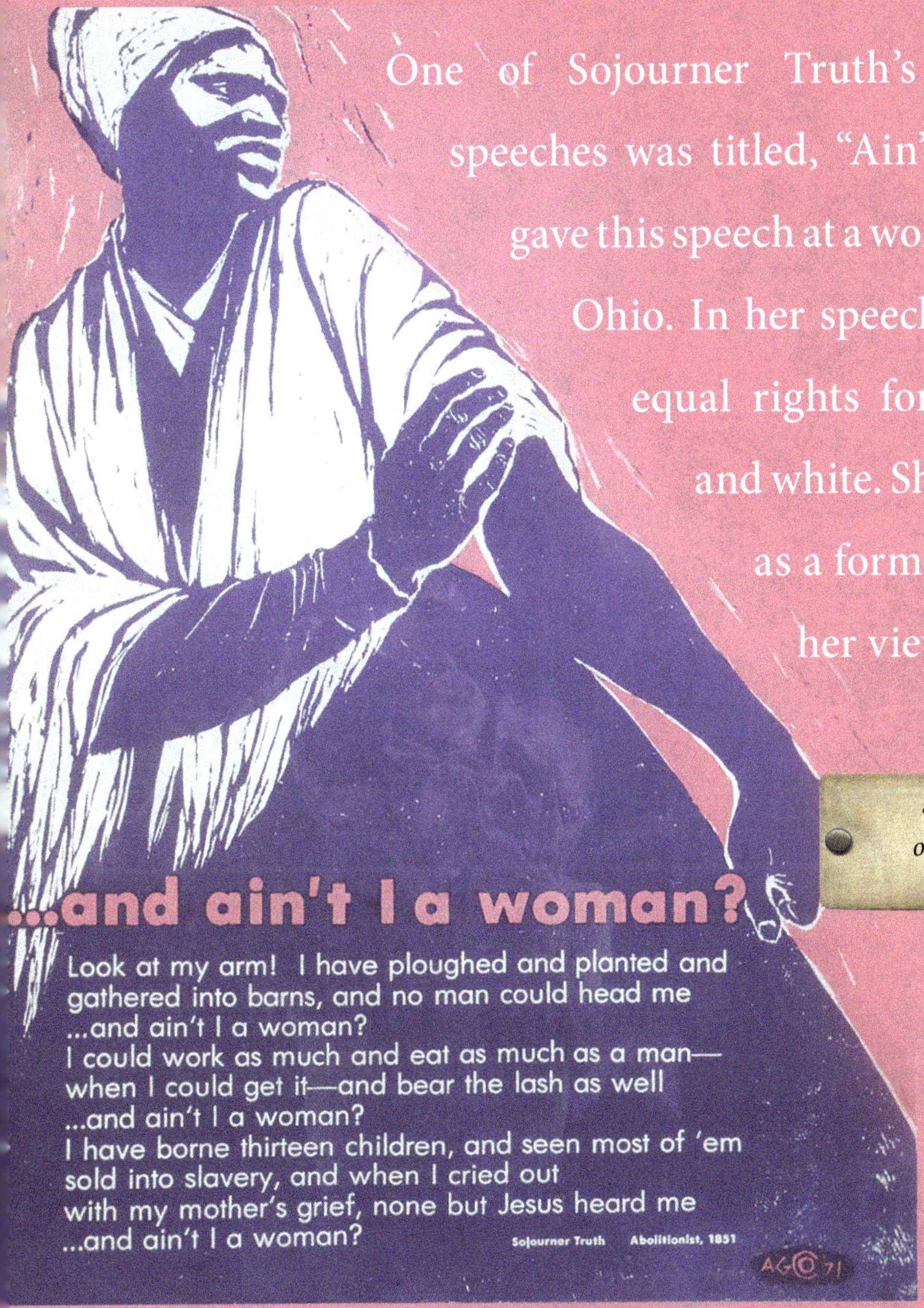

"Ain't I a Woman" was one of Sojourner Truth's memorable speeches.

Frederick Douglass's first autobiography, *Narrative of the Life of Frederick Douglass, an American Slave*, was published in 1845. It was so eloquently written that many people doubted that Douglass actually wrote it himself. Once word of his flowery speeches circulated, all doubts faded.

Frederick Douglass first autobiography.

Frederick Douglass

NARRATIVE

OF THE

LIFE

OF

FREDERICK DOUGLASS,

AN

AMERICAN SLAVE.

WRITTEN BY HIMSELF.

BOSTON:

PUBLISHED AT THE ANTI-SLAVERY OFFICE,

No. 25 CORNHILL.

1845.

Douglass presented himself as a sophisticated, educated, well-spoken person. He wrote two more autobiographies, *My Bondage and My Freedom* in 1855 and *Life and Times of Frederick Douglass* in 1881.

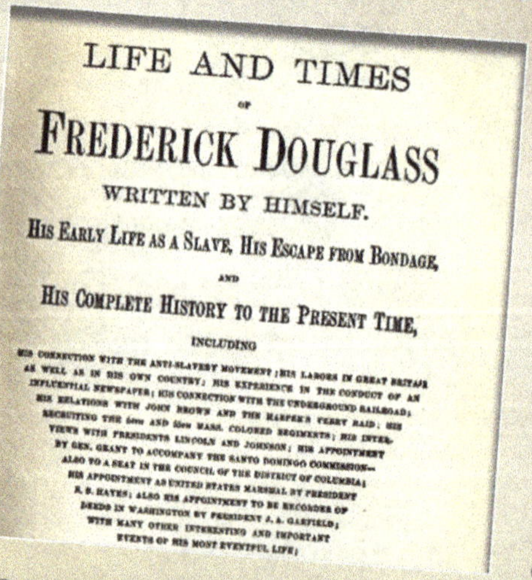
LIFE AND TIMES
OF
FREDERICK DOUGLASS
WRITTEN BY HIMSELF.
HIS EARLY LIFE AS A SLAVE, HIS ESCAPE FROM BONDAGE,
AND
HIS COMPLETE HISTORY TO THE PRESENT TIME,
INCLUDING
HIS CONNECTION WITH THE ANTI-SLAVERY MOVEMENT; HIS LABORS IN GREAT BRITAIN AS WELL AS IN HIS OWN COUNTRY; HIS EXPERIENCE IN THE CONDUCT OF AN INFLUENTIAL NEWSPAPER; HIS CONNECTION WITH THE UNDERGROUND RAILROAD; HIS RELATIONS WITH JOHN BROWN AND THE HARPER'S FERRY RAID; HIS RECRUITING THE 54TH AND 55TH MASS. COLORED REGIMENTS; HIS INTERVIEWS WITH PRESIDENTS LINCOLN AND JOHNSON; HIS APPOINTMENT BY GEN. GRANT TO ACCOMPANY THE SANTO DOMINGO COMMISSION— ALSO TO A SEAT IN THE COUNCIL OF THE DISTRICT OF COLUMBIA; HIS APPOINTMENT AS UNITED STATES MARSHAL BY PRESIDENT R. B. HAYES; ALSO HIS APPOINTMENT TO BE RECORDER OF DEEDS IN WASHINGTON BY PRESIDENT J. A. GARFIELD; WITH MANY OTHER INTERESTING AND IMPORTANT EVENTS OF HIS MOST EVENTFUL LIFE;

Frederick Douglass wrote two more autobiographies.

FREDERICK
DOUGLASS ABROAD

As Frederick Douglass became more well-known, he feared that his former slave master would come to reclaim him. In August of 1845, he left the United States to visit England and Ireland for a few months. Many former slaves relocated to Ireland. He wrote of his experiences abroad. He felt the weight of slavery and racial oppression lift from him.

Frederick Douglass Statue, Hornbake Plaza, Maryland.

Douglass noted that he could sit at the same dining table or in the same carriage with white folks and no one questioned it. Much later, after the Civil War, Frederick Douglass served as the U.S. ambassador to the Dominican Republic. This made him the first African American man to hold such a high office within the governmtent.

Frederick Douglass appealing to President Lincoln and his cabinet.

SOJOURNER TRUTH'S LIFELONG FIGHT

The abolition of slavery wasn't the only cause Sojourner Truth championed. She dedicated even more of her life to fighting for women's rights. In addition, she advocated for equality for all people, prison reform, and workers' rights. During the Civil War, she recruited freed African Americans to fight for the Union Army. She dedicated time to raise funds for the construction of hospitals for African Americans.

Sojourner helping people escape slavery.

More generally, she took steps to push for improved living conditions and employment opportunities for all African Americans. Although she remained illiterate, she dictated her life story into a book, *The Narrative of Sojourner Truth*. She lived off the profits from this book.

The Narrative of Sojourner Truth book.

OJOURNER TRUTH.

NARRATIVE

OF

SOJOURNER TRUTH,

A

NORTHERN SLAVE,

EMANCIPATED FROM BODILY SERVITUDE BY THE STATE OF NEW YORK, IN 1828.

WITH A PORTRAIT.

"Sweet is the virgin honey, though the wild bee store it in a reed;
And bright the jewelled band that circleth an Ethiop's arm;
Pure are the grains of gold in the turbid stream of the Ganges;
And fair the living flowers that spring from the dull cold sod.
Wherefore, thou gentle student, bend thine ear to my speech,
For I also am as thou art; our hearts can commune together:
To meanest matters will I stoop, for mean is the lot of mortal;
I will rise to noblest themes, for the soul hath a heritage of glory."

BOSTON:
PRINTED FOR THE AUTHOR.
1850.

SUMMARY

Both Frederick Douglass and Sojourner Truth were born into slavery but escaped to live in freedom. They used their experiences to advocate for the abolitionist movement. By sharing their experiences living in slavery, they helped more people understand why slavery needed to be abolished. Douglass and Truth devoted their lives to the causes they believed in.

For Douglass, those causes were abolishing slavery and promoting education among African Americans. For Truth, those causes included women's equality, workers' rights, and medical aid for African Americans, as well as ending slavery. They were both powerful and persuasive African American leaders who made an impact on history.

CPSIA information can be obtained
at www.ICGtesting.com
Printed in the USA
LVHW051246060423
743358LV00021B/471

9 781541 986435